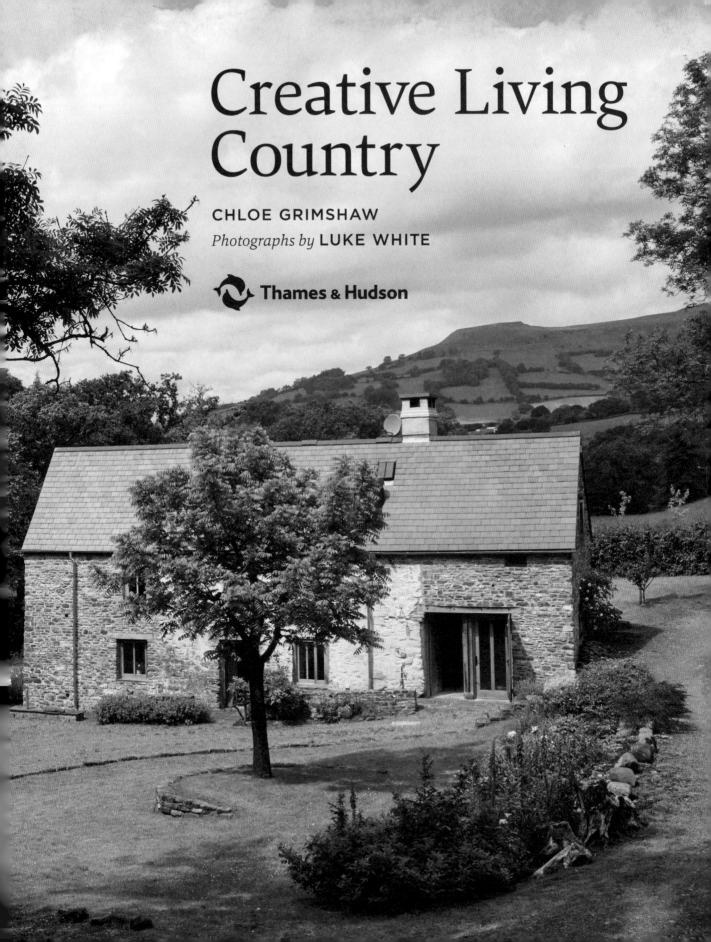

Creative Living
Country

CHLOE GRIMSHAW

Photographs by LUKE WHITE

Thames & Hudson

Contents

Makers

Designers

Creative Living

INTRODUCTION

Across the UK, artists, architects, makers and designers are choosing to make a new life for themselves and their families in the country. In leaving the frenetic pace of the city behind, they discover not only the space and quiet of the countryside, but also the mental freedom to pursue new ways of working.

Although this move to the rural idyll might seem like the ultimate in escapism, it is often a conscious, creative choice, made by those who have a living to earn, but want to do so in a way that feels more in tune with how they want to live or raise a family.

'Living and working here is more about a feeling of going within, rather than escaping from.'

HARRY CORY WRIGHT

Once they have made the move, these contemporary makers establish new studios, workshops and homes, but there is nothing traditional about their approach. The homes featured in these pages have been created from historic structures that have lain empty for centuries, from a martello tower (pp. 132–41) to a medieval chapel (pp. 142–53), or more humble buildings, including a mill cottage in the Brecon Beacons (pp. 110–21) and a garage in Norfolk (pp. 248–55), or even designed and built from scratch (pp. 122–31), but all have been transformed into inspiring places in which to live and work.

Beautiful countryside and seaside views can be found in the coastal towns of Kent and Sussex, just over an hour's travel from London, along with a huge range of affordable space. Further afield, in the midland county of Staffordshire and Cornwall in the southwest, the revival of Britain's traditional regional crafts adds to the lure of the countryside. It was this, along with the promise of more space for less money, which prompted ceramicist Reiko Kaneko (pp. 158–65) to swap her cramped Hackney studio for a spacious workshop in the historic Potteries. Rather than finding the move north to be a hindrance, she has found instead – along with many who have made a similar move – that her clients are happy to make the journey from London to visit her studio.

The steady rise in house prices has meant that many creatives are simply priced out of the London market, making the move out to the country a practical decision, as well as a personally fulfilling one. Studio space and rentals also tend to be cheaper, allowing young and emerging designers like Vanessa Battaglia and Brendan Young (pp. 276–85), Louise Body (pp. 256–65) and Jo Flowers (pp. 238–47) to base themselves in East Anglia and along the south coast.

But once there, how have these creative individuals made it work? The move out to the country can also mean a change in career. Jonathan Walter and Lakshmi Bhaskaran (pp. 218–27) left successful careers to retrain as furniture makers in Cornwall, and after Jo Pilkington (pp. 266–75) swapped her flat in Camden Town for a seven-bedroom Georgian house in Herefordshire, she also left the world of television and radio to set up 'glamping' business Mad Dogs and Vintage Vans.

The stories featured in *Creative Living Country* demonstrate that moving to the country isn't an impossible dream, or has to wait until retirement. The message to be gleaned from all of these creatives is that making the decision, taking the leap, requires courage and sometimes blind faith that it will work out. But once you do, and you find the life you dreamed of becomes a reality, the rewards are immeasurable.

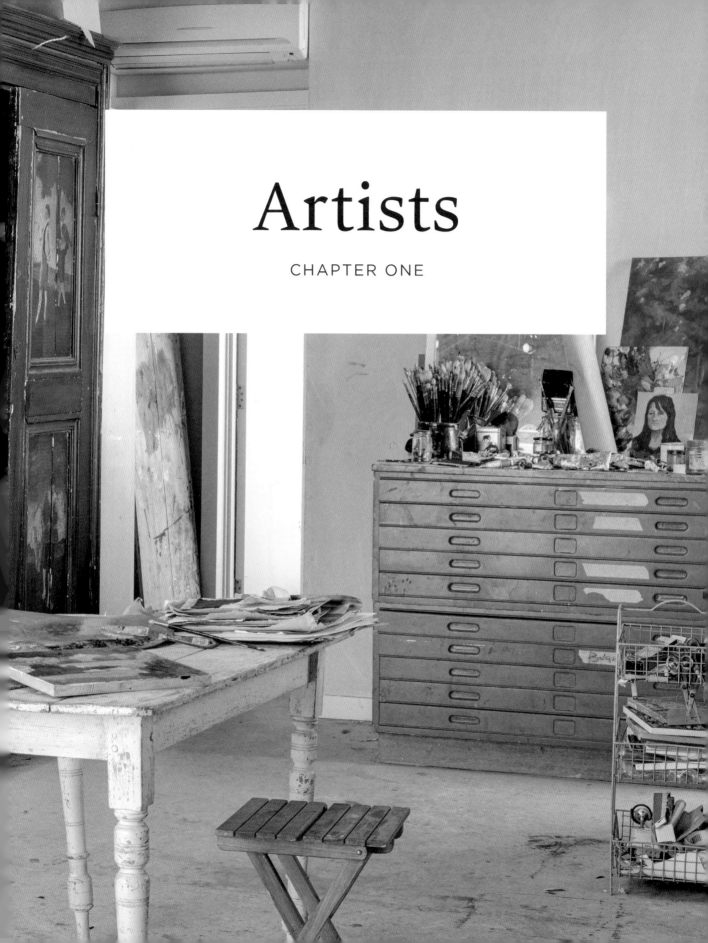

Artists

CHAPTER ONE

Artists have always had a pioneering spirit when it comes to finding and building a space to work in, whether moving into an empty warehouse or factory in the city, or converting farm buildings, garages, even houseboats in the countryside.

For Harry Cory Wright (pp. 68–75), this resourceful approach led to the conversion of an old pontoon in the Norfolk marshes into a drawing and photography studio. And when Ben Langlands and Nikki Bell (pp. 76–85) discovered an off-grid farmer's cottage in a field in Kent, they immediately knew that this remote spot would provide all the creative inspiration they might need.

In Somerset, photographer Matilda Temperley (pp. 58–67) returned to the family farm, a sprawling site in the Levels, and converted one of the barns into her photography studio. Daniel Chadwick (pp. 28–37) also returned to his family home, the Grade I-listed Lypiatt Manor bought by his father, sculptor Lynn Chadwick, in the 1950s. Keeping half the house as a gallery to display works by his father, himself and his wife Juliet, Daniel turned an outbuilding into a space for welding and metalwork. And in Suffolk, even the slurry house of a former dairy has been reconfigured as a painting and ceramics studio for Zara Chancellor (pp. 86–95) and her family.

Daniel & Juliet Chadwick

ARTISTS

As the son of sculptor Lynn Chadwick, artist Daniel Chadwick spent his childhood at Lypiatt Park in Gloucestershire, a Grade I-listed medieval manor house. Many of Lynn Chadwick's welded iron and bronze sculptures, including *High Wind III* (opposite), can be seen in the grounds of the house, which extend throughout the Toadsmoor Valley; his work is also in the collections of the Tate in London and the Museum of Modern Art in New York.

After Lynn's death in 2003, the house was left to the family. Later, Daniel bought out the remaining family members, and now lives and works in his childhood home with his wife Juliet and their own children, Caspar and Eva. Lynn had moved to Lypiatt Park in the 1950s, painting it white throughout and setting up a studio, complete with blacksmith's anvil, in the chapel.

Today, as well as owning the Woolpack Inn in Slad (of Laurie Lee fame), Daniel and Juliet continue to use half of the house as a gallery and studio space. Above the dining table is Daniel's *Little Pinky* (opposite), a mobile resembling swirls of air or liquid; in the hallway are two bronze figures by Lynn, *High Hat Man* and *High Hat Woman* (above). Suspended from the panelled ceiling is *Scorpion* (p. 32), another huge mobile. Daniel points to the terrazzo bathroom (p. 33) as evidence of Lynn's fascination with modern design: 'He was concerned with simple plumbing and ease of cleaning, and went a little wild here, which must have been quite an unusual thing to do in 1958.'

Perhaps unsurprisingly, Daniel has had a lifelong fascination with kinetic movement and mobiles. He began his career as an engineer, then joined Zaha Hadid Architects in 1987 as a draughtsman and model-maker, before leaving four years later to focus on his own projects. He describes his studio (pp. 34–6) as 'highly messy', and

is working on creating 'a private and special space, where the noisy and messy processes are separated'. Juliet, an artist herself, works in a converted hayloft, which can only be reached by ladder (p. 37). A slot in the floor allows her canvases to be moved in and out. 'It's a very private space,' Daniel says, 'and one of the nicest places in the whole complex, with a romantic balcony facing the morning sun.'

Daniel enjoys exploring the connections between art, design and engineering, and recent projects range from electric cars to pizza ovens, even sculptures inspired by Ordnance Survey maps. The translucent green *Wind Organism 1* (opposite) was designed to be the test-bed for his first outdoor pieces. 'Because the wind hits many pieces at once, it has an organic movement,' he explains, 'which varies from being reminiscent of a tree with leaves fluttering, to a swarm of bees or a shoal of fish. This is the holy grail for me,' he adds, somewhat ruefully, 'to recreate a shoal of fish.'

Ivor Braka

ART DEALER

For the past 30 years, art dealer Ivor Braka has divided his time between his home in Chelsea and an observatory tower on the Gunton estate in north Norfolk. He set about restoring the historic parkland at the age of only 30, with the help of architect Kit Martin and architectural historian Marcus Binney, and focused on the 18th-century designs of Charles Bridgeman, Humphry Repton and William Sawrey Gilpin. 'Luckily,' he says, 'we had maps of the original layout of the trees.' As restoration began, red and fallow deer were introduced back into the park, and the herd now numbers about 1,200.

When the local pub and hotel came up for sale in 2009, Ivor decided to buy the building. 'Pubs are closing down throughout England,' he explains, 'and I like to see thriving countryside communities.' Ivor's extensive art collection is displayed throughout the pub,

and some works have proved more controversial than others. In the 1980s, Ivor specialized in the work of artists such as Francis Bacon, Lucian Freud and Stanley Spencer, and has continued to focus on contemporary British art. Inside the bar and restaurant are works by Paula Rego, Tracey Emin, Julian Opie, Damien Hirst and Jonathan Yeo. A few pieces attracted complaints and were reported to the police, but Ivor remained firm and hired lawyers to assert his right to show a range of art. 'All of the work at the Gunton Arms is my personal taste,' he says – even if it is not to everyone else's.

The huge medieval fireplace and limestone flooring (pp. 44–5) were sourced from antiques dealer and decorator Robert Kime, as was the marble, rescued from Egyptian palaces during the 1920s, for the relaxed but still luxurious bathrooms (p. 46). Kime designed all of the bedrooms and bathrooms at Gunton. 'I really like the way Robert does things,' Ivor says, 'and I left the fabrics and furniture to him.'

Ivor wanted the pub and restaurant to look as if they had always been there, and was thrilled that artist Shaun Lavering was able to paint the bar 'so that it looked dirty and grubby' (p. 46). Prior to opening, Ivor turned to his friend, chef and restaurateur Mark Hix, for advice, who suggested one of his own head chefs, Stuart Tattersall, to head up the restaurant, with Stuart's partner Simone Baker managing front-of-house. Stuart was prepared to wait while Ivor completed the work, and joined as head chef and business partner in 2011.

From the start, Ivor was keen for the Gunton Arms to be welcoming to everyone. He sees it as a working pub, and enjoys the mix of people. 'You might get pig farmers mixing with people who look as if they should be sipping cocktails at Soho House,' he says. 'Seeing people queuing up to get in has been beyond my wildest dreams.' Having spent so many years restoring Gunton's historic parkland, Ivor has now created the perfect setting to enjoy it from.

THE OTHER RED MEAT

DEER

IT'S WHAT'S FOR SUPPER

IDAHO

2C C6731

Helen & Colin David

ARTISTS

Throughout the 1980s and '90s, the flamboyant designs of English Eccentrics were worn by everyone from Princess Diana to Mick Jagger to Prince. Launched in 1983 by Helen David, Judy Purbeck and Claire Angel (Colin joined the firm four years later), their designs are now in museum collections around the world, including the Victoria and Albert Museum in London and the Art Institute of Chicago. In 2013, they were featured in the V&A exhibition, 'Club to Catwalk'.

In 2005, some 20 years after first setting up English Eccentrics, Helen and Colin went back to school and enrolled in a printmaking course at the Royal College of Art. Today, they work as artists and textile designers, producing designs for the Scarf Gallery and the Christmas tree for the V&A, and divide their time between studios in King's Cross and north Norfolk.

In Norfolk, the couple live in an apartment in an 18th-century house, set over two floors and surrounded by parkland. The drawing room on the ground floor (pp. 50–1) reflects their bold approach to print and colour, with chartreuse-covered armchairs and a pair of purple-flocked candlesticks (p. 54). Although Colin and Helen feel the room is rather grand for their informal style, the mix of antiques and contemporary design is balanced by a characteristic wit and flair for colour, with tables covered with bunches of flowers from the garden in every hue imaginable (apart from yellow, which Helen has banned).

At either end of the drawing room are modern double-height additions, containing a large kitchen/dining space and a glass conservatory that doubles up as Colin's studio. The kitchen functions as an informal gallery space, with work by Helen providing the only splash of colour against the white-painted furniture and cream crockery (above). Upstairs are bedrooms for the couple and their two children, along with guest bedrooms.

Just glimpsed through the conservatory is *Tangled Love* (opposite), a heart of red-flocked antlers by Colin, which was inspired by the 18th-century deer park nearby. An artists' residency in Spain also proved fruitful, and resulted in a red fan in the sitting room (p. 52) and a silkscreened skull in the guest bedroom (opposite). Print curtains by Helen show the couple walking in the deer park (p. 54); in the bedroom is *Silver Sovereign*, a Pollock-inspired portrait of the Queen (p. 55).

New work is displayed in every room, and the couple regularly move things around to best showcase their latest creations. The garage has been converted into a – sometimes freezing – print studio (above and opposite), and Colin and Helen cheerfully admit to wearing boiler suits while working in the winter. Having returned from a trip to Rajasthan in northern India, they are back at work, getting ready for an upcoming publication and exhibition of their latest designs.

Matilda Temperley
PHOTOGRAPHER

'I've always been a wanderer, living out of a suitcase,' says award-winning photographer Matilda Temperley. But when her family farm in the Somerset Levels was flooded in 2013–14, and her grandfather was one of the first people to be evacuated, she decided it was time to return home. The Temperley family, fifth-generation farmers who run the Burrow Hill Cider Farm, near Martock, helped out as much as they could, using their tractors to traverse flooded roads and wading across fields to check on neighbours. Roads and homes remained under water for 63 days before the waters began to subside.

Matilda photographed the disastrous effects of the flood, and the results were gathered in her self-published book *Under The Surface: Somerset Floods*, which won the Royal Photographic Society's Vic Odden Award

in 2015. The following year she received the Joan Wakelin Bursary to fund her ongoing work in Ghana to document leprosy (Matilda trained as a scientist at the London School of Infectious Diseases, specializing in tropical diseases such as leprosy, dengue and river blindness).

When she moved back to the farm, Matilda converted one of the outbuildings into an office and photography studio. 'I've never collected things,' she says, 'and I am finding it quite hard to fill up the space.' A pair of sofas were spotted under a sign reading 'free to a good home', and the kitchen was picked up on eBay. Matilda's sister, fashion designer Alice Temperley, supplied the cushions and the mirror ball (pp. 60–1). To take a break from editing and computer work, Matilda practises her circus skills with the help of a hoop and some aerial silk she has hung from the rafters.

Matilda's parents have supported local farmer Michael Eavis, founder of the Glastonbury Festival, from the very beginning, and

each year the whole family travel to Worthy Farm in a handpainted
bus. 'My parents are both very creative, and when we were growing up,
we always had unusual people living at the farm,' Matilda explains.
'People who lived life on their own terms.' Perhaps this is where
her fascination with performers began: Matilda has photographed
aerialists and performance artists for most of her life, and celebrates
them in her third book, *The League of Exotic Dancers*.

When she is home at the farm, Matilda prefers to camp out in the
garden in a mud house with a grass roof, a log cabin with a wood-
burning stove or a gypsy caravan. 'There's always something new to
do here: harvesting, pruning, pressing cider,' she says. 'It's never boring
or monotonous.' Travelling around the world, she adds, has made
being at the family home even more precious. No matter how torn
she feels about being on the road or working in London, 'nowhere
else in the world really matches up to Somerset.'

Harry Cory Wright
PHOTOGRAPHER

'Being on the houseboat feels as if you are at the centre of everything,' says Harry Cory Wright, whose photographs of the coastline of Britain and Ireland were published as *Journey through the British Isles* in 2007. Harry often describes this stretch of the north Norfolk coast as where his fascination with the changing landscape began, over 20 years ago.

In 1990, Harry had been given the chance to renovate an old wooden pontoon, near the village of Brancaster Staithe, which had been used by the local waterskiing club – and he jumped at it. Gradually, he cleaned out the mud, repaired the hole and opened out the rooms to create a large interior space that functions as living room, bedroom and kitchen, with views of the estuary (overleaf). This leads to a small hallway and bedroom with four built-in bunk beds at the opposite

end, overlooking the marshes. Jackets, bags and camera equipment are hung from hooks on the door (above), along with the coils of rope (p. 75) used to moor the boat at low tide.

'In the early days, we lived on the boat and I based my work here for many years,' Harry says. 'Within 10 minutes, you are taken to another world,' he continues, describing the extraordinary feeling of looking out the window and being entirely surrounded by water. As the tide rises and falls the marshland gradually disappears, replaced by a floating world. During the summer months, Harry will often begin work at dawn to capture the sunrise and early light. By the time he stops for breakfast, he has already completed a full morning's work.

When the children came along, Harry and his wife Miranda decided to move to a cottage in Burnham Market, just around the corner, but they still love camping out together as a family on the houseboat. As it had been somewhat patched together over the years, Harry decided to

commission sculptor Fionn Rawnsley to rebuild the top of the
boat and the interiors, following the previous footprint in 2009.
The hull was rebuilt by canal-boat fitters in Nottingham.

Having recently begun to make ink sketches of the marshes,
Harry has found himself intrigued by the relationship between
his photographs and drawings. Over the past few years, he has
begun to work in a much looser way, working with a small black-
and-white handheld camera and making drawings of the coastline
from memory. He showed his drawings for the first time in 2016,
and produced a new book, *Marsh*, to accompany the exhibition.

Over the past 10 years, Harry's travel photography has taken him
around the world, with commissions from *Harper's Bazaar*, Chanel
and the BBC, but he still stubbornly returns to work at his small
Norfolk houseboat. 'I like the transient nature of the landscape,'
he says cheerfully, 'where the same thing never happens twice
and the creeks and tides swirl around like a big washing machine.'

Ben Langlands
& Nikki Bell

ARTISTS

'We had been to see Derek Jarman's house in Dungeness and stumbled on this place by accident,' explains artist Ben Langlands, describing the moment he and Nikki Bell discovered the site for their off-grid house in Kent. The couple loved the idea of living in the Weald, an area of outstanding natural beauty in southeastern England, but recognized the challenge of taking on a dilapidated farm building with no mains electricity or water.

As Turner Prize-nominated artists, Ben and Nikki's practice covers sculpture, film and video, digital media and architecture. In 2004, the year they were nominated for the Turner Prize, the couple collaborated with structural engineers Atelier One on the Paddington Basin bridge. Keen to work with them again, they employed the firm to help prepare the drawings and obtain planning permission.

Having always wanted to build a home from scratch, Ben and Nikki's designs became a balancing act between respecting the beautiful landscape of the Weald and making the house work as efficiently as possible, including fitting solar panels at a lower angle. Mindful of environmental sustainability, the couple also chose a prefabricated building system for the main structure, which was delivered and erected in less than two weeks. They project-managed the build themselves, living on-site in a shipping container.

'Untitled', as the couple call the house, is only an hour away from their Whitechapel studio, so Ben and Nikki can easily divide their time between London and Kent, depending on work and the time of year (they prefer to be in the country during the summer to make the most of the long daylight hours). Luckily, it was a fast build, and the couple were able to move into the house after only one winter in the

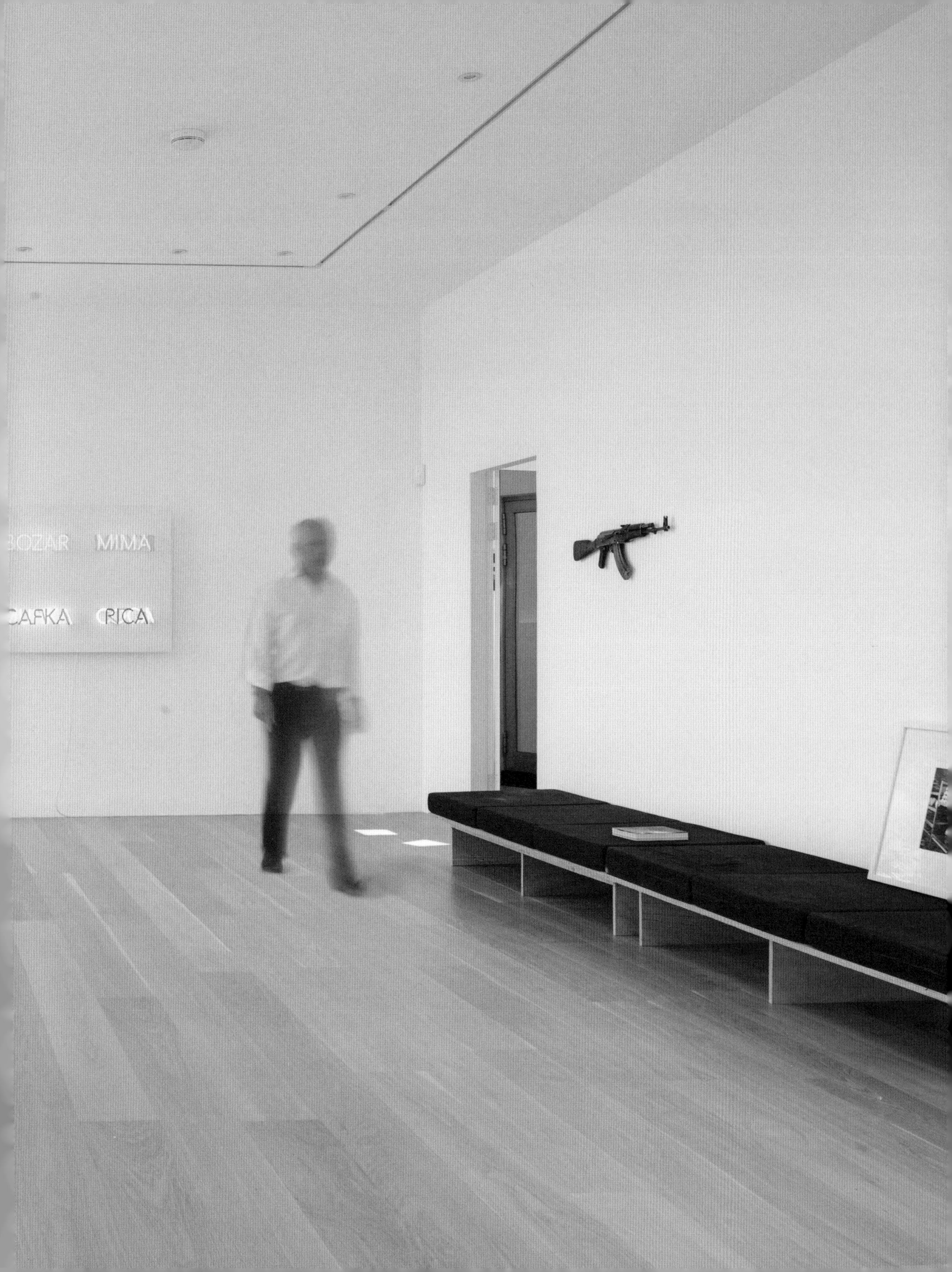
BOZAR MIMA
CAFKA RICA

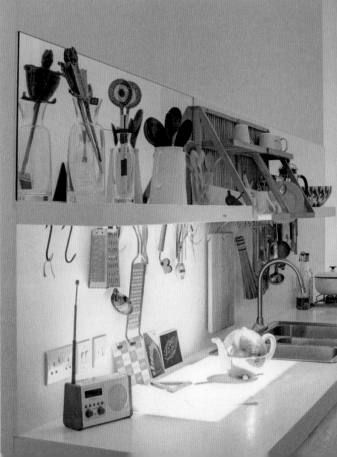

container. Now that the house is complete, they have embraced life in the country, buying produce from the local farmers' market and jam from the Women's Institute, and often cooking on the wood-burning stove, which generates enough heat to warm the entire house on all but the coldest days. The only jarring note in this idyllic scene is provided by the AK47 on the wall of the living room (opposite), a commission for an exhibition held in 2012 to mark the International Day of Peace.

In their quest to achieve total immersion in the countryside, the couple planted a hedge of hawthorn, blackthorn, dog rose, field maple and guelder rose around the property. With views out over the fields beyond, and no other house in sight, 'Untitled' is now the perfect antidote to urban living. 'The whole of the summer is extraordinary,' says Nikki. 'And because we're off-grid, it's a fantastic feeling to think that everything here is generated by the sun.'

Zara Chancellor

PAINTER

When artist Zara Chancellor came across a steel and brick barn on the Stour estuary in Suffolk, built in 1927 as a dairy to supply the staff and students of the Royal Hospital School with milk and butter, she was eight months pregnant and her future home was still a shell. But Zara and her husband Charlie loved the location, where the quality of light and huge skies have been a source of inspiration to artists from Thomas Gainsborough and John Constable to Paul Nash.

Once the couple took on the project, they were keen to respect the industrial character of the barn, while also creating a warm, family home. Only minimal changes were made to the layout: the bullpens were transformed into three bedrooms and a bathroom, and the first-floor grain store became two guestrooms and an office for Charlie.

At the centre of the building is a large kitchen and living space, with floor-to-ceiling windows and views over the sheltered walled garden and fields leading down to the river. Bold tiles from Emery & Cie provide a graphic splashback (opposite), while a 17th-century French table and 1950s Danish dining chairs complete the look. The couple spent many years collecting antique furniture and lighting, trawling the Golborne Road market in London. Some of these treasures include the Gio Ponti-designed armchairs in the living room (overleaf and p. 95) and the vintage painted cupboard in the studio (p. 94).

Zara worked closely with architect Katy Woollacott (whose own house is featured on pp. 110–21) to bring unusual colours and textures into the barn, including shimmering gold silk wallpaper, which covers one wall of the dining room and brings much-needed light and warmth into the tall, narrow space. Zara loved the effect so much that

she chose to leave the wall completely empty, with just one painting in a gold frame (p. 88). Similarly, Zara felt that with the 25m (82 ft)-long installation by Devon-based ceramicist Jacob van der Beugel (above) stretching along one entire wall in the living room, there was no need for further adornment. With the bookshelf and other furniture in the room all quite low to the ground, bringing in any other element would merely distract and simply wouldn't work.

Zara's approach to designing her new home was to think of it in the same way as 'making a painting, and thinking about composition, with negative and positive in perfect balance'. She wanted to avoid traditional ways of living and was keen for her home 'to challenge you out of your comfort zone'. All of this was only made possible by the strong working relationship Zara had forged with her architects, and the trust she placed in them. 'They didn't just build a house for us,' she says, 'they gave us a whole new way of life.'

Architects

CHAPTER TWO

Childhood dreams of castles, towers and forts have come true for this group of architects, who have designed their own castles in the country with magical results. Ruined buildings that have lain empty for years – sometimes centuries, as in the case of Duncan Jackson's martello tower (pp. 132–41), originally built as a coastal defence during the Napoleonic wars, in Suffolk, and Charlotte Boyens and Adam Scott's 11th-century Norman chapel in Pembrokeshire (pp. 142–53) – have been rescued, reimagined and restored as innovative family homes.

Rich in historic significance, too, is a lighthouse in Winterton-on-Sea, in Norfolk (pp. 100–9). Having bought it on April Fool's Day, Sally Mackereth later discovered that it is mentioned in Daniel Defoe's tale of shipwreck and survival, *Robinson Crusoe*. More humble structures have also benefitted from an architect's vision, as Katy Woollacott and Patrick Gilmartin cleverly transformed a simple mill cottage into a building that fits into the local vernacular (pp. 110–21). By adding extensions at either side, they turned a small building into one approximating a Welsh longhouse, with room for three generations. Elsewhere in Wales, a new build designed by Sarah Featherstone and Jeremy Young (pp. 122–31) is as imposing as its predecessors. Called Ty Hedfan ('hovering house'), it appears to float above the river.

Sally Mackereth
ARCHITECT

Together, Sally Mackereth and her partner, creative director Julian Vogel, are known for their pared-back aesthetic. In 2013 Sally set up Studio Mackereth to explore new sculptural and tactile designs for jewelry and furniture. This interest in colour, space and volume has found physical expression in the couple's holiday home, a lighthouse on the northeast coast of Norfolk. Wanting to provide an old-fashioned childhood for their two young children, Oscar and Lola, they started the search for a countryside bolthole.

Sally, however, couldn't see herself living in a traditional cottage, and began to look at chapels and schoolhouses along the east coast. Eventually, she spotted an ad for a dilapidated lighthouse. It was undeniably romantic (and even mentioned in *Robinson Crusoe*), but the lantern had long since disappeared. Feeling

that the building simply didn't look enough like a lighthouse, Sally
began sketching ideas in her diary. With a new lantern installed,
the lighthouse is once again a much-loved local landmark, and one
neighbour even says that the sight of it 'makes my heart sing'.

Before the family moved in, the building had to be made as
comfortable as possible, a challenge Sally saw as a complicated jigsaw
puzzle that 'needed to be unpicked'. Bunkbeds are built into the curve
of the walls (p. 106), with a winding staircase leading to the master
bedroom above and an almost vertical, ladder-like set of steps reaching
from the circular library to the sleeping platform at the top (p. 109).
A wood-clad extension contains the large living space (p. 104), with a
wood-burning stove and furniture by Dutch designer Cees Braakman.
At the bottom is the wraparound kitchen, along with the bathroom
(p. 107). Here, Sally was inspired by the original beams to clad the
whole of the room in wood panelling, which was then painted white.

The glass 'cabinet of curiosities' in the living room (p. 108), once used for French patisserie, now contains 'stories of the lighthouse and the sea', including a piece of the concrete 'lid' built by the army during the Second World War to protect the lighthouse from bombs. Also among the treasures is one of the nuts that once bolted the lantern to the roof and a brass button from a coastguard's jacket.

The Norfolk coast is a constant inspiration for Julian, whose ceramics are influenced by 'those big vast skies'. Window ledges, bureaus and shelves are home to his hand-thrown stoneware (above and opposite). 'No two pieces are the same,' he says, 'but I like the way a collection of objects reads – there is a symmetry that I find really pleasing.' Sally also finds inspiration in her surroundings. 'To be relaxed is a much more creative state to be in,' she says. 'If I need to take a step back and think, I will bring work here, but never a laptop.'

Katy Woollacott
& Patrick Gilmartin
ARCHITECTS

With three generations of one family living under one roof, this small mill house in a quiet Welsh valley needed an overhaul to suit all of its residents, aged two to 72. Fortunately, architects Katy Woollacott and Patrick Gilmartin have always run their business from home, so when they set out to create a home for themselves, their three children and Katy's parents, they were already well versed in the delicate art of balancing work and family life.

The mill house dates back to the 16th or 17th century, although little remains of the original building. To help them envision how the house could be remodelled to suit their needs, the couple studied old photographs and were immediately struck by how few possessions people had. They expanded on the idea of storage that was integrated into the structure by extending the studwork out

to form shelving a pantry, a hallway, even a bathroom. Because they also wanted the house to remain in keeping with its setting, Katy and Patrick added extensions at each end to replicate, in effect, a Welsh longhouse. They used stone from the nearby river (above), with its characteristic rounded edges that necessitate fat mortar joints and create a slightly untidy appearance, a detail that Patrick particularly likes.

On the ground floor huge doors and windows open out onto swathes of green beyond (previous pages), creating an almost seamless transition between inside and out. The kitchen faces Crug Hywel, or 'Table Mountain' (opposite), with views of the sunset, while the living room (overleaf) looks down the garden towards the river, which can be heard rushing past below. A new wooden staircase winds around the existing chimney and leads up to three bedrooms on the first floor, with a narrow staircase continuing up to the rooftop

space with four single beds (above). Katy was keen to echo the vivid greens of the countryside in the textiles and soft furnishings inside the house, and her extensive collection of vintage Welsh blankets also help create a cosy feel that is miles away from their busy life in London.

The finish was kept deliberately rough, with unpainted sawn oak used throughout (opposite). The wooden detailing has been left unpainted, and timber windows have been allowed to turn silver with age. On the upper floors, the couple chose to keep the existing small windows, rather than replace them with larger ones (p. 120). 'I was absolutely fascinated by small windows, because you imagine yourself inside peering out onto the landscape,' explains Patrick. 'It's like a little frame or a picture, focusing you in a moment of time.'

Sarah Featherstone
& Jeremy Young
ARCHITECTS

Despite living and working in East London, Sarah Featherstone and Jeremy Young seize every chance they can to escape to the Brecon Beacons mountains in South Wales, where Sarah spent childhood holidays. In 2010 Ty Hedfan, meaning 'hovering house', became the first project the couple completed together. Situated in a wooded valley, the house appears to hover above the river, hence its name.

The site slopes down to the confluence of two rivers, Ysgir Fach and Ysgir Fawr, which flow across the length of the property. The design allows for wraparound views of the river and surrounding hills, and the house was intended as a place where Sarah and Jeremy could relax and catch up on work. Despite the presence of a separate study, the couple gravitate towards the kitchen table – also designed by them, with 'Compass' trestle legs

by Matthew Hilton (opposite) – with its beautiful morning light and views across the valley. To ensure the house is energy-efficient, solar panels and an air-source heat pump were installed, along with a green roof. The whole project was overseen by Osborne Builders, a family-run business based in Builth Wells, using locally sourced materials.

The rough-hewn wall of the hall staircase, made from Welsh stone, creates a wonderful counterpoint to the smooth stairs in vivid shades of green that echo the valley beyond (p. 123). To unify the interiors with the outside space, natural hardwood was used for the windows and kitchen surfaces (p. 128). The units are from Ikea, and their brightly coloured doors were built by furniture designer Dominic Ash, a friend of the couple. In the living room (overleaf), Sarah and Jeremy also opted for high-street designs, including sofas by Muji, which were covered in Sarah's collection of Welsh blankets and textiles designed by Eleanor Pritchard.

For the dining room, Sarah discovered some good copies of
Ercol chairs on eBay. She also invested in the real thing, with a pair
of 'Dowel' chairs by Charles and Ray Eames and a Donna Wilson-
designed pouffe for the living room. Not everyone would want an
open-plan pink bedroom and bathroom (opposite), but the couple
couldn't resist having a custom-designed bathroom in rosy tiles and
Corian with a corresponding carpet in the bedroom. 'Designing for
yourself is very liberating and allows you to be more experimental,'
explains Jeremy. 'Being able to do both is a great opportunity.'

Ty Hedfan was recognized with a RIBA Award in 2011, and the
couple continue to design environmentally friendly homes and award-
winning new buildings. Recent projects include Waddington Studios,
a former board-game factory in Stoke Newington, North London,
which won a RIBA Award in 2015, and a revamp of the interior
office space for advertising agency Wieden + Kennedy in Spitalfields.

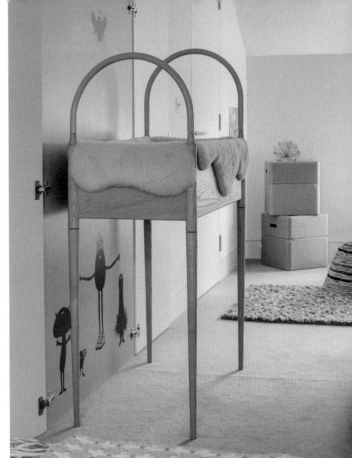

Duncan Jackson

INDUSTRIAL DESIGNER

Duncan Jackson first came across his future home nearly 20 years ago, while out walking with friends. One of three martello towers on a shingle beach in Suffolk, it was in poor condition with grass growing on the roof. Duncan later discovered that two of the towers belonged to a local farmer, who invited him for lunch – the start of a long friendship – and agreed to sell him one.

Built during the Napoleonic wars as part of the country's coastal defences, Tower Y's thick walls were designed to withstand cannon fire. Around 140 martello towers were erected in all, mostly along the southeast coast. These imposing buildings, up to 12m (40 ft) high, would have been accessed via a ladder through a door hovering over 3m (10 ft) off the ground. 'Peeling back the building and working out how to do it took time,' says Duncan.

Although work began in 2002, the complications of renovating
a waterlogged listed building meant that work wasn't finished until
eight years later. As an industrial designer, Duncan was keen to be
involved at every step, and worked with architects Piercy Conner (now
Piercy & Company) to decide how best to convert the building. 'We
explored it without any preconceived ideas of what a home means,'
he says. 'The nature of the building seemed to offer a blank canvas.'

Now complete, the building is a striking, and unusual, home. At the
top is a kitchen, with a glass roof enclosing the raised platform and
a central pivot (still in place) for a cannon. Duncan wanted a robust
fit-out for the kitchen, in keeping with the character of the tower, and
commissioned a bespoke curved stainless-steel counter and circular
kitchen island (overleaf). He had made the kitchen table himself (for

his wedding lunch in 2007), but gave his designs for the beds and
the sofa to Italian furniture-makers Poltrona Frau. Below the kitchen,
the living space is illuminated by narrow slits in the wall, originally
for defensive musket fire. This huge area would have accommodated
24 soldiers and one officer, with fireplaces for cooking and heating.
Bedrooms were relocated to the ground floor, with the main bedroom
converted from the magazine (opposite); the other storerooms would
have been used for ammunition, water and provisions.

Duncan's wife Kristin is a gallerist and curator, and shipped over
their wonderful collection of prints, books and ceramics from her
former home in Lake Michigan. Their daughter Lily was only 18
months old when the family moved into the martello tower, and has
grown up in this extraordinary circular space. 'As soon as children
come inside, they start running around,' Duncan explains. The grown-
ups, however, tend to gravitate to the top floor of the tower for the
hypnotic views of the sea and the Suffolk countryside.

Charlotte Boyens & Adam Scott

ARCHITECTS

'We always have an eye out for interesting buildings,' says architect Charlotte Boyens. 'Each of us has that dream that one day we will find an ancient stone building and convert it into a home.' Having met as students at the Royal College of Art, she and partner Adam Scott have done just that with an ancient stone chapel in the Welsh countryside, which they now share with their two sons, Albion and Oren, and their parents.

As their London flat was only 100m² (1,076 sq ft), with no garden, the couple, who work as 'experience architects' at FreeState, the company they set up with Ben Johnson in 2003, began looking for a holiday home with plenty of space for the boys to run around in. Adam and his mum had been looking for a place in Pembrokeshire, where they had spent family holidays when Adam was a child, and

143

stumbled upon an 11th-century Norman chapel. After getting a
builder to check that it was structurally sound, Adam and Charlotte
bought the property online, without even visiting it. 'I was quite
desperate to work on something like it,' says Charlotte, 'knowing
it would be there for decades, if not hundreds of years.'

The couple loved the chapel's simplicity, and chose a restrained
palette of colours and materials to prevent it feeling too cluttered.
Ironwork from the altar rail was reused to make side tables for the
living room, placed next to sofas in ecclesiastical purple (opposite).
Dividing the space proved to be the main challenge. A double-height
timber wall was installed, with two doors leading to the staircase,
utility room, bedrooms and bathroom. The Norman font, beneath an
arch separating the former chancel and nave, is the centrepiece of the
building. To create the kitchen and dining area, the altar was lowered
and the top replaced with a new piece of oak to form a work surface.

The dining table was made by a local metalworker, and the 'Wishbone' chairs are a classic design by Hans Wegner (pp. 146–7). Charlotte, especially, loves them, noting that their oak frames and woven seats feel both contemporary and traditional.

Before construction could begin, a new home had to be found for the resident bats, so the couple built a large wooden shed with an attic for the bats and enough space below for a workshop (p. 153). The boys each have their own workbench, and Adam, who trained to be a stonemason in between his architectural studies, has begun to teach them the basics. The family has also thrown themselves into the outdoor life, surfing up the estuary and fishing from the beach. 'The only sad bit was coming home to London,' Albion says, 'when we realized that this adventure was nearly over.'

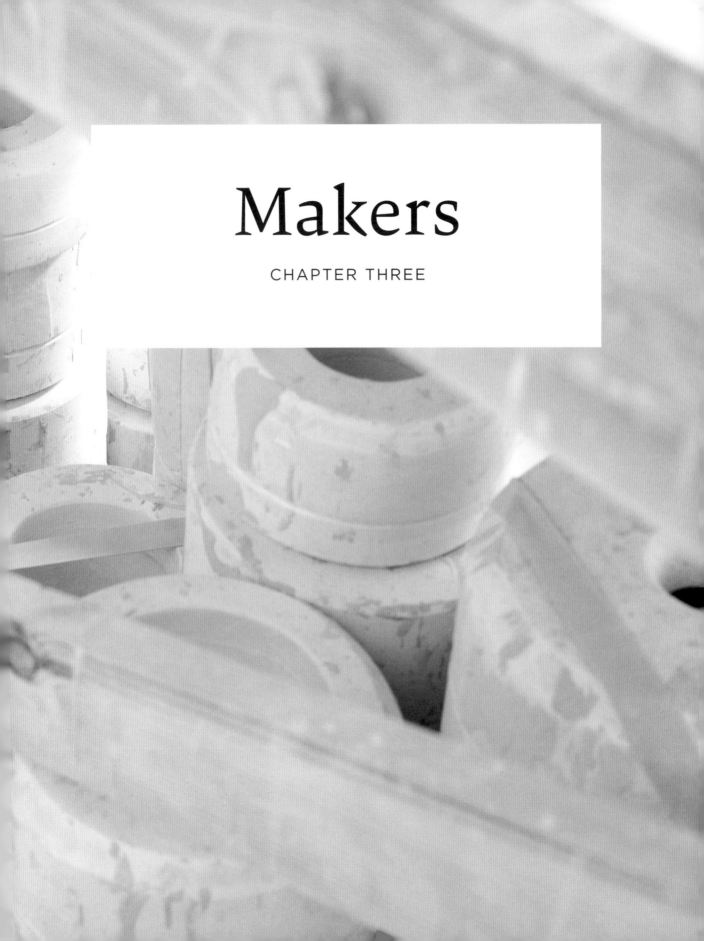

Makers

CHAPTER THREE

Rather than rejecting age-old British crafts like boat-building, clockmaking, pottery and cabinetry, contemporary makers are embracing the work of previous generations, and paying homage to the skill that went into producing it.

Ceramicists Camila Prada (pp. 206–13) and Reiko Kaneko (pp. 158–65) both moved to the heart of Britain's historic ceramics industry to learn from local makers, while passionate sailors Greg Powlesland (pp. 176–85) and Luke Powell (pp. 196–205) headed to Cornwall to build careers as shipwrights. Both endeavour to preserve traditional building techniques, with Greg restoring classic yachts and Luke designing pilot cutters based on 19th-century designs.

In Somerset, At The Chapel (pp. 186–95) in the middle of Bruton High Street has always been at the centre of local life. Originally an abbey, then an inn and finally a chapel, the building was eventually turned into a hotel and restaurant by cabinetmaker Ahmed Sidki and his wife Catherine. And in Wales, Chloe and Jim Read (pp. 166–75) have bucked the trend: rather than moving to the country, they never left. The couple set up the highly successful Newgate Clocks, designing and producing clocks and watches not far from their hometown of Oswestry in Shropshire.

Reiko Kaneko

CERAMICIST

Having spent her childhood in Japan, Reiko Kaneko is fascinated by its ancient traditions and rituals, but also loves contemporary design, fuelled by her studies at Central Saint Martins in London. Working from a studio in Stoke-on-Trent in Staffordshire, the centre of Britain's pottery industry, Reiko produces her ceramic designs in delicate bone china and collaborates with companies such as SCP, for whom she designed a lighting range and the 'Orlando' chair, her first piece of furniture.

In 2012, Reiko decided to leave the busy, vibrant London borough of Hackney and move to Stoke-on-Trent, keen to learn more about the area's connections with ceramics. Initially, she rented a light-filled studio in one of the town's many Victorian industrial buildings, but has since expanded into the downstairs space; the decorative details on the ceiling are left over

from its former life as a plaster-cast showroom (pp. 164–5). 'Having this space has allowed me to experiment with glazes that are special to bone china,' she says, noting the generosity of the local suppliers who introduced her to new glaze techniques.

Within a year, Reiko also found a cottage to rent, 10 minutes from her studio and located in an idyllic mill setting with extensive gardens, which can only be accessed via a footbridge that crosses a stream alongside the property (p. 163). Roger the turkey arrived in time for Christmas, but now roams free in the garden. Inside, Reiko displays apple blossom in her own ceramic designs, following the principles of *ikebana* (opposite). 'You hold each stem in front of you,' she explains, 'turn it around and consider its beauty and the aspects you'd like to display, before carefully placing it in the vase.'

'I am drawn to natural materials, and anything that ages well,'
she continues, pointing out a green bottle vase by Dutch maker
Klaas Kuiken (above) and works by Munakata-sensei, a potter from
Fukushima-ken, where Reiko grew up. Recently, she visited the Bizen
pottery in Japan and was intrigued by the traditional kilns, which give
the pots their characteristic finish, as if they had been 'licked by fire'.

Once a week, Reiko practises *kyudo*, an ancient form of Japanese
archery (opposite). Her home is filled with *kyudo* references, from fans
to paper targets, and she admits that if she lived in Japan, this would
become a daily ritual. Her home is a visual world, but one where the
tactile is as important: she brings home grains of sand from her travels,
and the cottage is criss-crossed with rough wood beams. She collects
works of art that are handmade, including glass and ceramics, but
most importantly 'anything that reminds me of a place and time'.

Chloe & Jim Read

CLOCKMAKERS

Chloe and Jim Read launched Newgate Clocks in 1991, in their hometown of Oswestry, Shropshire, inspired by the great British brands of the 1950s and their own collection of vintage and antique clocks. With orders flooding in from stores across Europe and the US, the couple spent the next 15 years on the road. 'That transformed the business,' says Jim. 'You are quite closeted living in Wales, and then you travel to the great cities of the world and soak it all up.'

'Everyone thought for years that we would never make a go of anything,' adds Chloe, 'but then it all clicks.' Twenty-five years later, the couple still design and produce all of their clocks in Oswestry, working from an ex-Laura Ashley factory they purchased in 2009 and filled with 1940s desks and vintage lighting, creating new studios and display areas.

The couple previously lived in a small cottage in a damson orchard, just outside Oswestry, followed by an old vicarage in the countryside, before eventually deciding they needed a larger house, so that their three children (Ruby, Buster and Lola) could each have their own room and Jim could work from home two days a week. When they discovered a double-fronted Georgian house in the centre of Shrewsbury, complete with oval staircase and large garden (p. 175), they snapped it up.

Every part of the house needed modernizing, along with new plumbing and electrics, but Chloe and Jim took on the project as the original detailing was still intact. With a contact book of antiques dealers amassed over the past 25 years, they also roped in their parents and Chloe's brother (all antiques dealers themselves) to search for furniture, lighting, glass and ceramics, and purchased larger items on eBay. Drawn to items that are as functional as they are beautiful, the

couple gravitated towards 20th-century industrial pieces from
factories and science labs, along with vintage shop fittings, all of
which their parents, collectors of Victorian and Georgian antiques,
considered 'a load of junk'. The couple have had the last laugh,
however, as today these items are hugely collectible.

To fill their vast house, the couple needed to get creative. Jim
used shop fittings for the kitchen (opposite), and placed two display
units together – a glass counter with brass detailing and a cosmetics
display unit – and topped both with a slab of Carrara marble to make
a kitchen island. He also designed the chandelier that hangs above it,
using four antique glass globes. The creative process tends to happen
around the dining table (pp. 170–1): a huge mahogany oval table
picked up at Newark Antiques Fair in Nottinghamshire, with plenty
of space to spread out with samples and drawings. The children
also help out with designing clocks and watches, 'including a rabbit
watch', says Jim, 'designed by Lola, aged eight.'

Greg Powlesland

SHIPWRIGHT

Having studied art at St Martins School of Art (now Central Saint Martins) in London, Greg Powlesland has carried on drawing and sketching throughout his life. His other great passion is sailing, and it was when travelling down the coast from Saltash in southeast Cornwall over 30 years ago that he discovered his future home on the Helford River. He has dedicated his life to restoring old boats and houses, and today there is almost nothing that he can't rebuild with his bare hands.

In 2002, Katie Fontana, co-owner of bespoke kitchen company Plain English, sailed *Zircon* into Gweek Quay boatyard for repair and struck up a conversation with Greg about boat-building and craftsmanship in general. They became a couple, and now divide their time between Cornwall and a houseboat in London. Their first project together was to restore

Patna, a 17m (55 ft) yacht from 1920. Although the original detailing was mostly intact, restoring her became a six-year project. Today she is moored in Cannes, and the couple sail her around the Mediterranean.

Greg's home, built in 1927 on the banks of the river, partly on stilts to accommodate the 30° slope, proved to be similarly challenging. When he discovered it in the 1980s, it was little more than an overgrown shack. The National Trust tried to buy it, but the owner, a local farmer, preferred Greg's philosophy of rebuilding the house using local and reclaimed materials. First, Greg pulled down the garage and started again, focusing on building the new studio and workshops. The new building now contains the bedroom, bathroom (above), living room (previous pages) and kitchen in one wing, with the studio and workshops in the other two wings, creating a U-shape.

The double-height studio links the living space to the workshops for metalwork, woodwork and stone carving. In the centre of the wood workshop is the deckhouse of a steamship, which Greg discovered in pieces in a car park. 'The ethos is about using good-quality reclaimed materials,' he explains. 'It is a labour of love.' Katie has her own design studio in an old Pullman carriage in the orchard (opposite, top left). The couple have now turned their attention to the original house overlooking the river, with Greg redesigning the space and adding a slate roof and Katie working on the interiors.

When the 120-year-old buoy at August Rock, near the entrance to the Helford River, needed to be replaced, Greg contributed towards a new one (which was funded by public subscription) and was able to keep the original. It now sits proudly at the entrance to the property (opposite, top right), and is a daily reminder of how the river has shaped so much of this couple's life and work.

Ahmed Sidki

CABINETMAKER

Having lived in Notting Hill in West London for over 30 years, cabinetmaker Ahmed Sidki and his wife, restaurateur Catherine Butler, began to spend weekends in Bruton, Somerset. They bought a derelict Grade II-listed chapel as a retreat, camping out in different parts of the building as they did it up whenever they were down. Everything needed replacing, from the floors and the roof to the electrics and the plumbing, and weekends became longer and longer, sometimes stretching to four days.

After six years of commuting, the couple made the decision to live in Somerset full time, running a bakery and restaurant in the chapel, which had originally been Ahmed's studio. Initial planning consultations took place in 2006, and it was another two years before the new venture, called At The Chapel, was able to open. Ahmed designed all of the architectural

detailing, from the spiral staircase (pp. 194–5) to the chapel doors and the wood-fired bread oven, and employed the local blacksmith to make the cast-iron handrails and door handles. The final step was to commission *Faith* from sculptor Lucy Glendinning, which now hovers above the restaurant (p. 194).

Ahmed has always been closely involved with Catherine's restaurants, designing all the tables for her first restaurant in Notting Hill over 20 years ago, as well as for At The Chapel. Here, the arched door (p. 186), leading to the bakery and wine shop, remains open throughout the summer. Beyond is a double-height space, which has been converted into the restaurant. The Bruton branch of art gallery Hauser & Wirth is just down the road and holds regular exhibits here; Ahmed and Catherine also host their own events, including exhibitions and readings, in the clubroom on the lower ground floor. Even the Royal Ballet has performed here. An abbey originally stood

on the site, followed by the Swan Inn in the 17th century, which was rebuilt as a chapel two hundred years later. The couple moved out of the chapel in 2013 (which was then converted into an eight-bedroom hotel) to a cottage in the village, with wooden beams and low ceilings, which Ahmed then converted into a modern home with clean lines, white walls and high ceilings.

The cottage is now the perfect space in which to display Ahmed's collection of contemporary and mid-century paintings and ceramics from his former gallery, Bowwow, in Notting Hill. In the bedroom is a triptych by outsider artist Jesse Leroy Smith, while a charcoal drawing by Richard Allen hangs in the hallway (p. 188). Ceramics range from delicate, bird-like shapes by Vivienne Foley to huge, coiled vessels by Abigail Simpson (p. 191). The Calder-inspired mobiles, wooden dining table and sculptural bronze bench were all designed by Ahmed (pp. 189, 190).

Luke Powell
SHIPWRIGHT

Messing about in boats has always been in Luke Powell's blood. 'In 1969, when I was nine,' he says, 'my parents bought an old fishing boat and dumped the three of us, along with the dog, the cat and the canary, on the boat, and we went off to Greece.' The family lived on the boat for the next 20 years. Luke's father gave him an old sailing boat to fix up, and by the time he was 22, he was ready to take on his own restoration project.

Along with boat-building, Luke also worked as an artist, and eventually swapped his paintings for a boat of his own. He sailed to France, where he built fishing boats for the next six years, until his marriage ended. Luke then sold up and moved back to England, and in 1997 Classic Sailing, a holiday company in Cornwall, commissioned him to build his first pilot cutter, *Eve of St Mawes*.

This marked the beginning of a 20-year love affair with pilot cutters, and Luke has now built eight of them, including the 14m (46 ft) *Agnes* in 2003, based on a design from 1841 and along the lines of the historic pilot cutters from the Isles of Scilly. Today, Luke and his wife Joanna sail her around the Cornish coast and Scilly, and even across the channel to Brittany and Galicia, in the northwest corner of Spain.

Following the financial crash in 2008, the couple set up a charter company, Working Sail. Known for his somewhat gruff reputation, Luke claims that the boatyard staff told him it would never work because he would hate the people. In fact, Luke admits, 'the people' have proved to be the most fascinating part of the whole exercise. 'Everybody has a story to tell,' he says, 'and the worst thing is that they might be slightly boring. Half the time it's like sailing with friends.' Seven guests sleep in wooden bunks at the front of the boat (above and opposite), while Luke and Joanna sleep at the back, behind the kitchen.

For those that wish to drink aboard ship
Bottles of Wine can be purchased at
£9

For those that wish to read
Take a Book can be purchased at
£30

'I've always been good at making things with wood, so I thought if I had the raw material, I could add value to it in some way. We built it up from there.'

LUKE POWELL

'Once you are away on a trip,' says Joanna, 'everything calms down and you get into the rhythm of being on the boat, slowing down and taking your time.' She cooks for crew and guests, using the tiny cooker on board, and somehow produces roast chicken and loaves of freshly baked bread. The weather tends to dictate meals. 'If it's really stormy,' she says, 'we eat a lot of stew and bread.' On calmer days, the couple and their guests fish off the side of the boat and eat what they catch. Everyone eats on deck, and no one goes down below except to sleep.

Joanna is a great admirer of Luke's skill and passion for boat-building, but admits: 'He lives and breathes boats, and I don't want to do that. There are other things I want to do.' Balancing work with home life and looking after her 12-year-old son can be difficult, and she admits that she sometimes envies the seemingly perfect lives of the guests. With everyone sharing a small space, however, she finds that it can all come pouring out. 'It is a bit like a therapy boat,' she says.

Camila Prada

CERAMICIST

Having launched her hugely successful online business in 2010, today Camila Prada works from a studio attached to the Gladstone Works in Stoke-on-Trent, Staffordshire, which dates back to the 18th century and still has the original bottleneck kilns that are so characteristic of the region.

Her home is a top-floor flat, sandwiched between two grand Victorian buildings: the Burslem School of Art and the Wedgwood Institute. It is perhaps no coincidence that she has made her home in Burslem, one of the six towns amalgamated to form Stoke-on-Trent in 1910 and where Josiah Wedgwood was born. As a graduate of Staffordshire University's Ceramic Design MA programme, Camila has always viewed Wedgwood as an influential figure in her work, citing both his innovation in design and his entrepreneurial spirit.

After graduation, Camila began working at Rosenthal (owned
by Wedgwood) in Germany in 2006, and released a new range of
products under their 'Thomas' label of colourful tableware. When
Wedgwood went into administration in 2009, so too did Rosenthal.
At the time, Camila heard about a new festival in Berlin called
'Pictoplasma', which celebrated contemporary character design. She
stayed for two nights and loved the modern, edgy feel of the festival.
'It was extremely creative,' she says, 'with a cute/ugly aesthetic that I
wanted to put into ceramics.'

When Camila won a commission from the Black Country Museum
in nearby Wolverhampton, she decided to relaunch her company, but
this time selling directly from the Internet, rather than from stores.
Her new work was well received, but she found that she had trouble
with her kiln. 'To have a clean and consistent look is very difficult,'
she explains, 'the room has to be clean, with no dust and a consistent

'Everyone told me
that I needed a shop.
But I thought, why
not promote my
designs online?'

CAMILA PRADA

temperature.' She met with small factories, of no more than five to ten employees but who could make thousands of pots each day. After three tries, she found the right one, but it took many years to find a factory that could work with her relatively small order.

Innovative design and social media have been key to Camila's success. Perhaps surprisingly, she prefers not to design on the computer, and instead uses paper cut-outs or draws directly onto the object. Each collection consists of a limited edition of 200, in seven different designs, totalling 1,400 pieces. In 2016, she invited her followers to pre-order from her new collection on Facebook, and 350 people registered in the first week. Camila finds that her customers often share their stories on social media, not just about contemporary design, but also about the experience of childhood or even of becoming a parent. Her work has tapped into a certain kind of nostalgia for beautifully made, handcrafted children's toys, made in Britain but with a contemporary edge.

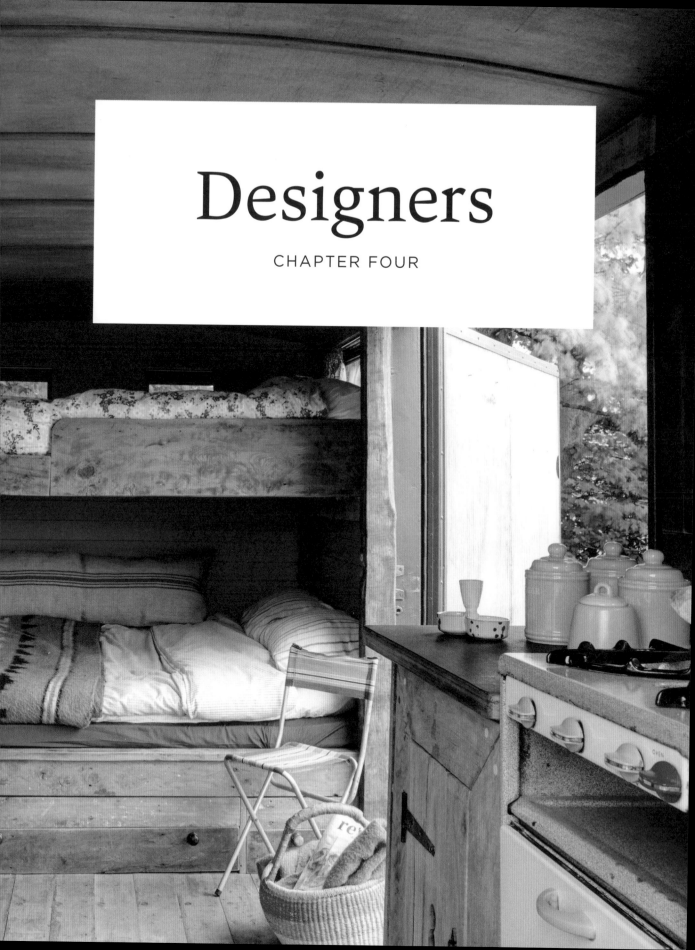

Designers

CHAPTER FOUR

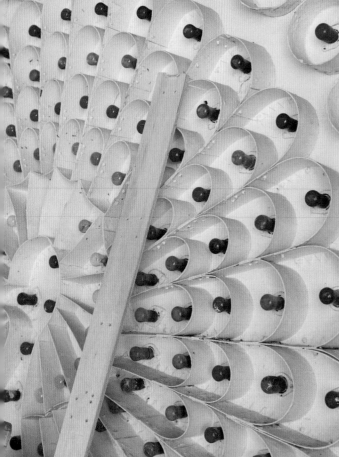

Traditional country pursuits, from camping in the great outdoors to the art of flower-arranging, are being reimagined as careers for the 21st century. In Herefordshire, Jo Pilkington (pp. 266–75) has upgraded camping to 'glamping', and introduced a new generation of campers to the joys of crumpets around the campfire, while in Norfolk, Jo Flowers (pp. 238–47) has channelled her childhood love of gardening into a thriving business, gaining 50,000 followers on Instagram in the process.

The seaside has also been a draw for creatives including Phil Oakley (pp. 228–37), who restores vintage illuminations and designs new ones in neon at his studio in Hastings. Fellow Hastings resident, wallpaper designer Louise Body (pp. 256–65), also finds inspiration in her surroundings, with the colours of the sea and sky feeding into her own watercolours and work for other designers, among them Paul Smith and Stella Jean.

For others, including furniture designer Lisa Whatmough (pp. 248–55), the move to the country means an escape from the workday week. Her bolthole on the Norfolk coast has no television or wi-fi to distract from the soothing sounds of the waves crashing on the beach below. But the creative spirit is still very much in evidence, however, as her designs can be seen in every room of the cottage.

Jonathan Walter & Lakshmi Bhaskaran

FURNITURE DESIGNERS

Six years ago, Jonathan Walter and Lakshmi Bhaskaran arrived in Cornwall from Notting Hill, in a vintage VW camper van filled with surfboards, to set up their bespoke furniture business Bark. Now they are married with two small children, Indira and Ajay, a thriving business and a new home – but, unfortunately, not as much time for surfing.

The couple met while studying at the Rowden Atelier furniture school in Devon, taught by master craftsman David Savage. Lakshmi gave up her career as a design writer for titles such as *Wallpaper** magazine (she is also the author of five books on the subject) to become a furniture designer-maker. Jonathan had also had another career, working in the City before taking up surfing and furniture-making in São Paulo in 2002, and finally returning to the UK in 2006.

'I haven't been back to
London for two years,
and there is nothing
that I miss.'

LAKSHMI BHASKARAN

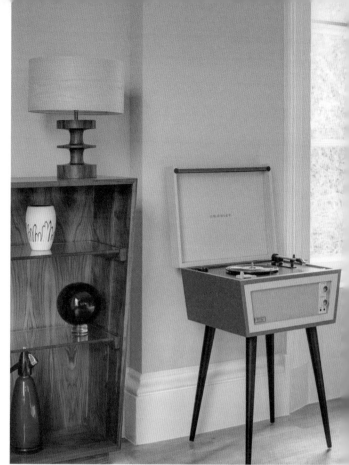

The couple set up home in the small town of Stratton, just outside
Bude, in what was originally the old rectory, built in 1830 and later
divided in two (their lucky neighbours occupy the other half, where
The Beatles allegedly stayed in the 1960s and scratched their names
into the window). It still has the original front door step, a huge slab
of slate, worn down over the centuries. Previous extensions provided
an extra floor, as well as a light-filled corner living room.

Lakshmi and Jonathan have made very few alterations to the house,
beyond painting it white throughout and adding an orange carpet,
which runs 'like a ribbon' through the building (p. 225). The objects
on display neatly encapsulate the evolution of the London design
scene, from a Marc Newson-designed dish drainer to a concrete rocking
chair by Willy Guhl (previous pages) and a 'Jack' light by Tom Dixon.
The couple's own creations for Bark reflect their love of mid-century
design, and can be seen at Wahaca restaurants in London, Bull Hotels
in Spain and Jimmy's Famous American Taverns in California.

Other designs by Lakshmi and Jonathan include a writing desk and chair (below), elegant armchairs and coffee tables (p. 222), and high-chairs for the children (p. 223). Preferring to invest in contemporary design or make their own furniture, rather than buy vintage, the couple furnished the living room with a treasured lamp from the 1960s by Achille Castiglioni and a Matthew Hilton-designed sofa, which sits next to one of their own 'LoMo' sofas for two in vivid green (pp. 220–1).

With their workshop only five minutes away, the move to Cornwall has allowed the couple to achieve the perfect work-life balance, with Jonathan able to be home for the children's bath and bedtime at six, before heading back to the workshop. And now that Bark's unique take on design has been rewarded with international recognition, making the leap to living in the countryside begins to look less like a whimsical idea and more like a sound business decision.

Village fetes, surfing on
the school curriculum,
beachcombing in the sunshine
– these are all compelling
reasons for bringing up
children in Cornwall.

Phil Oakley
ILLUMINATIONS

After a project involving the reinvention of Blackpool's famous illuminations fell through, lighting designer Phil Oakley and his partner Olivia left the northeast and moved back to London. Once there, however, they struggled to find a showroom, workshop and living space that was big enough to display Phil's vast collection of neon. When a friend suggested St Leonards, part of the town of Hastings in East Sussex, Phil spotted a derelict pub in an online auction. The couple made a low offer via sealed bids, and were somewhat taken aback when it was successful.

Having become the owners of the former Admiral Benbow, the couple were then faced with the daunting prospect of renovating it. The building was filled to the brim with sofas, piles of clothes, fridges, bottles and empty crisp packets. Before they could even think about

designing the space, Phil and Olivia had to clear it out, which seemed
to take up every single weekend. Once the space was emptied, Phil
researched the building at the local library, and discovered that it was
originally a coaching inn, the Saxon Shades, which dated back to 1833.

The couple created a double-height living and dining room with a
skylight (overleaf), and converted a corner bedroom into a sitting room
with a view of the sea. The ground floor is now the workspace and
showroom, with the living spaces, kitchen and bathroom on the first
floor and the two bedrooms at the top. Before installing his collection
of illuminations, Phil wanted to make sure that the building was both
efficient and safe, and installed new fire doors, electrics and plumbing,
as well as thermal and sound insulation.

The couple have commissioned work from local artists and
designers, including handmade wallpaper from Deborah Bowness
(above) and an ornate mosaic skull from Susan Elliott (Roger Daltrey
of The Who is another fan). Citing the success of the family-run Links
Signs, a specialist sign company that produces all of the signs for
London Underground, Phil feels that there is plenty of potential
for larger-scale creative and tech businesses to move to the area.

With his own business growing, Phil has also taken on a commercial
building in Hastings to store his illuminations (p. 228), hiring a local
sign-painter to decorate the outside. And as the couple become more
at home in this corner of East Sussex, they have realized they are no
longer just part of a gang of creatives, but part of a wider community
– a feeling reinforced by the arrival of their two cocker spaniels, Jarvis
and Joe Cocker (p. 230). 'When you stroll along the beach,' says Phil,
'everyone stops to talk to you.'

Jo Flowers

FLORIST AND STYLIST

Ten years ago, Jo Flowers decided to make
a career out of her childhood passion for
gardening and enrolled in a floristry course
at her local college. From the start she
championed a more natural approach to
floral arranging, and has now become part
of a large network of florists and growers via
social media. When *Harper's Bazaar* named
Jo as one of their top 20 florists for 2013, her
career blossomed, and she now has nearly
50,000 followers on Instagram.

Jo is a third-generation gardener: her
father kept an allotment in Norfolk, while her
grandparents had the 'most beautiful garden
in Suffolk, with a showy, floral front garden
and a back garden for vegetables'. She started
out working for florists in Norwich, but found
their approach too formal and soon began to
make bouquets and wreaths for the Christmas

and summer fairs in Southwold and Bungay, in Suffolk. To achieve the
naturalistic look of her bouquets, she mixes in wildflowers, such as
daisies and foxgloves, as well as creepers, vines and honeysuckle.

Jo lives in a Victorian gardener's cottage, originally part of the
Colney Hall estate in south Norfolk, which also included a village,
parish church and extensive parkland. Her children all live at home:
son Lucas; Lola, an interiors stylist; and Molly, a veterinary student.
Molly and her partner Jimmy help tend the garden and look after the
large flock of prize-winning rare-breed ducks and chickens, including
a handsome Golden Brahma rooster (p. 245) and Gorgeous George, a
Barley duck who won first prize at the 2013 Royal Norfolk Show.

Over the years, the brightly painted interiors have gradually become
more muted, with natural linens and whitewashed furniture acting
as a backdrop to her floral creations and bouquets. The living room,
kitchen and study are on the ground floor, as is a large conservatory

(p. 238 and overleaf), where Jo works. Bedrooms and bathrooms
are upstairs, with a guest bedroom also on the ground floor (above).
Works by local artist Kate Nicole and Jo's twin sister Nicola Rodwell
are propped on shelves or leaned against walls or beds – nothing is too
formal here. Jo's collection of vases is 'ever growing', as is her collection
of cream ceramic Fulham vases and bowls from the 1920s to the '40s
(p. 241). Favourite haunts include the nearby Diss Auction Rooms, but
she is equally happy rummaging in skips. The jug on the kitchen table
(previous pages), found at a car-boot sale, is a favourite and loved by
Jo for its shape and texture.

When Jo first moved to the cottage, one of the first things she did
was to plant new borders with rare and unusual varieties of roses and
dahlias. In the spring, she works on the dahlia and sweetpea gardens,
and in the autumn plants out her bulbs. Only January and February
offer the chance for a well-earned rest and time to plan the year ahead.

DO NOT MOUNT THE DEER

Lisa Whatmough

DESIGNER

As the head of bespoke furniture and design company Squint, launched in 2005 and with a client list that includes Stella McCartney and Mario Testino, Lisa Whatmough seizes every opportunity she can to escape to her seafront bolthole on the Norfolk coast. Most Fridays, Lisa can be seen heading north from her home in Hackney, arriving in just over two hours.

Once there, it is all about simple pleasures: taking a mug of tea outside to sit on the sea wall (opposite), tending her garden or walking her beagle Stanley on the beach. Lisa admits to struggling with the garden, with the coastal winds putting paid to more delicate plants, but kindly neighbours have given her cuttings from their own gardens, and she has had some success with irises and red hot pokers. On Sunday, she packs up and is back in London by lunchtime, ready for the week ahead.

Perched on a cliff and resembling a clapboard New England house or quirky English beach hut, the cottage is in fact a clever conversion of an old garage, and was a holiday let before being reinvented by Lisa. Huge picture windows overlook the sea, with the waves crashing just a few feet below. Everything is open plan, apart from the bedrooms and bathroom, and painted in Farrow & Ball's Cornforth White, a soft, soothing grey. The wood-panelled snug (above) provides a separate, cosy space, with 1950s wall lights adding to the cocooning feel.

Most of the furniture was covered in Squint fabrics especially for the cottage, from the sofabed in the snug to the four-poster bed from Ikea (p. 253). Some of Lisa's earliest pieces were home accessories like teapots, which she wrapped in fabric by hand, and she has recently begun to commission lighting from a marble studio in the north of England, to which she adds lampshades of her own design (opposite).

In East London, where her studio is based, Lisa is part of a close-knit design community. When it came to choosing pieces for her weekend cottage, she turned to furniture-makers Unto This Last for the dining table (above and opposite), and picked up a rug from Caravan, a shop owned by her friend Emily Chalmers. (The white-and-gold pendant light above the dining table was a housewarming gift from Emily.) Among Lisa's most treasured pieces are the shell lights in the snug, made by the studio that produced Picasso's sculptures.

As the house was meant to provide a complete break from work, Lisa chose not to have connections fitted for TV or broadband. But she loves having friends and family to stay and isn't precious about her furniture designs, although she does notice that children can't resist touching them. Staying in her house is a bit like living in a sweet shop, with the treasures on display too beautiful to resist.

Louise Body
WALLPAPER DESIGNER

Wallpaper designer Louise Body shares
her home in Hastings, East Sussex, with
her husband Jonny, who also manages her
business, and their children Isaac and Marney.
She is part of a new generation of creatives
based in and around Hastings, including
Phil Oakley (p. 228), fellow wallpaper
designer Deborah Bowness and Andrew
Hirst of vintage fabrics company Wayward,
and firmly believes that the colours of the
sea and sky have filtered into her work.

Having launched her wallpaper designs to
great acclaim in 2003, Louise spent the first
year screenprinting them by hand. Demand
quickly outstripped supply, and she moved
production to a wallpaper factory in the
north of England, where her designs are
still produced today. Her work is now in the
permanent collection of the Victoria and

Albert Museum, and she continues to work from her studio in the St Leonards area of Hastings, just behind the seafront and a short walk from the town's distinctive black-painted Net Shops (p. 256). A recent collection, 'Paper Tiles' (p. 257), combined photographic trompe l'oeil with intricate drawings to create the feel of vintage tiles in a range of muted colours. These proved to be so inspirational to Haitian fashion designer Stella Jean that she invited Louise to design the runway, invitations and lookbook for her Spring/Summer 2014 collection.

The family home has provided Louise with a backdrop for her experiments with new designs. The house itself is painted in soft blues and greens, inspired by the colours of the seaside, and reflected in wallpaper patterns including 'Old Blue' and 'Chalk Tile', which are wrapped around the kitchen (p. 260, below). Wall murals including the bold, 1960s-inspired 'Poppy Tree', also designed by Louise, hang above a mid-century sideboard in the living room (p. 260, above).

'I love the space you get looking out to sea. It makes me feel calm, and is somewhere I can collect my thoughts.'

LOUISE BODY

From her grandparents, who owned a design shop in Southend
in the 1960s, Louise inherited a collection of glass and ceramics,
including the Murano glass egg-timer in the kitchen (opposite) and
the blue vase in the bedroom (above), where her 'Abstract Wall' mural
provides a backdrop to more textile designs, including 'Dot To Dot'
quilts and 'Celestial Sky' cushions. A vintage lace dress hanging on
the wall is another treasured item from her grandmother.

Scouring the local shops produced the display cabinets in the dining
room, one of which Louise sanded down and painted (p. 258), and the
elegant wall sconces, picked up at Butler's Emporium and rewired by
her neighbour, Phil Oakley. The Ercol armchair (p. 259) was an eBay
find and is upholstered in 'Peggy', another of Louise's designs. Living
by the seaside has provided inspiration for her work and a wonderful
way of life for the whole family. 'In the summer, we are in the sea and
on the beach every day after school,' she says. In the winter, we go
down to the shore for the crashing waves and sense of exhilaration.'

Jo Pilkington
VINTAGE CARAVANS

After 18 years of working in television and radio, Jo Pilkington was ready to leave London behind and make a fresh start in the country with her family. She and her husband Al Farquhar, who had worked in the music industry for many years, began exploring the Somerset and Herefordshire countryside, and soon discovered a Grade II-listed Georgian rectory near Ross-on-Wye. 'Once I walked through the front door and into the sitting room, with its perfect proportions and spectacular views,' says Jo, 'that did it for me.'

With the couple and their three daughters settled in, Jo began looking for ways that would make the new house pay for itself and also allow her to be a full-time mum. Outside the school gates she met fellow mum Sacha Morley, who was renovating a caravan (named 'Elsie') but had nowhere to put it. Once Jo mentioned

that she had a wildflower meadow alongside the house, the idea for the 'glampsite' Mad Dogs and Vintage Vans was born. With neither of them natural campers, Jo and Sacha were determined to create a comfortable, luxurious experience, with fairy lights, lanterns and candles adding to the magical atmosphere.

Recycling and restoration is at the heart of the campsite's philosophy. Of the vans available to stay in, 'Gertie' is a Cheltenham Gnu, one of only two in the country, and dates back to the 1930s, with purple upholstery and a pale-pink curved ceiling (p. 267). 'Monty' is an ex-military vehicle, built in the 1970s to a Second World War design (pp. 274–5). Well known on the West Country rave scene, it was discovered at auction, painted orange and covered with stickers. Now repainted a more sedate shade of green, the van's interiors were also transformed, using wood and slate to create a cosy space, complete with bunkbeds and a wood-burning stove.

Inside the house, Jo replaced the vintage wallpaper only where necessary, using designs by Neisha Crosland (opposite, below right) and a silver foil wallpaper by Anna French in the breakfast room (pp. 268–9), which shimmers in the morning sunshine. The sideboard and refectory table were left by the previous owners, while the gold-framed portrait is from Jo's mum and the baby grand piano was inherited from a neighbour (p. 271). The sitting room, with its wonderful view, is Jo's favourite space in the house. In the bathroom (opposite, above right), sanded-down floorboards from the old office were reused as panelling.

Spending more time with friends and family on outdoor adventures or around a campfire sounds like 'the stuff of dreams', Jo admits, but it has proved to be essential, both to her family and the many guests who come here 'to get away and unplug' from stressful, busy lives, reconnect with nature, sit around an open fire and watch the sun set over the Black Mountains. 'If you don't seize your chance, you may never do it,' she says. 'Having young children gave me that chance.'

make one thing a day
- BUY LESS (MAKE MORE)
- CONSUME LESS
- DRIVE LESS
- WALK MORE (EXERCISE MORE)
- COOK MORE
- UNPLUG MORE
- SLEEP MORE
- BE MORE OUTDOOR
- DO ONE THING AT THE TIME
- ADD SLOW movements and RITUALS INTO DAILY SCHEDULE
- DO LESS
- WANDER MORE (DISTRACTED thinking is replaced with intuitive contemplation)
- DO MORE YO YUU (momentary pause to recharge and to arrange mental clutter)
- BE MORE ALONE
- BE more with family AND FRIENDS

Vanessa Battaglia & Brendan Young

DESIGNERS

Tucked away down a quiet side street on the outskirts of Cambridge is an unassuming 1970s house. Inside, it is inspiring and highly original, filled with the designs of Vanessa Battaglia and Brendan Young, who set up the Mineheart studio in 2010. The couple design lighting, furniture, rugs and cushions, and regularly collaborate with new designers, including Angela Rossi and Simon Schubert.

Vanessa and Brendan have prototypes and samples dotted around the house, which, they explain, help them 'understand ourselves and our designs better'. The couple recently collaborated with Chiara Fersini of Himitsuhana on a new collection of rugs and surreal still-life canvases, one of which hangs above the sofa (p. 283), while her Geisha-inspired 'Repose' rug has pride of place in the bedroom (p. 280).

Tackling their small house, with its boxy rooms and low ceilings, was a challenge. The couple papered the kitchen and living room with an 'almost white' wallpaper to open out the space. With a blank canvas established, they allowed Gothic elements to creep in, including owls, skulls and lamps made from black feathers (above). Working on a tight budget, they found the two Chesterfield sofas and a vintage workbench on eBay, and converted the latter into a kitchen worktop.

Just around the corner is Brendan's father's workshop. Outside is a 'recycling shelf', where people can leave unwanted items for anyone to take away – including Brendan and Vanessa, who found their pale blue garden table here. Above it is a painting of pink peonies by Vanessa's father (p. 284). Design is always personal for this couple, with Brendan's tiny childhood chair (a present from his grandfather) and old wooden toys on display in their son Antonio's room, against 'In The Clouds' wallpaper, the couple's own design (p. 282).

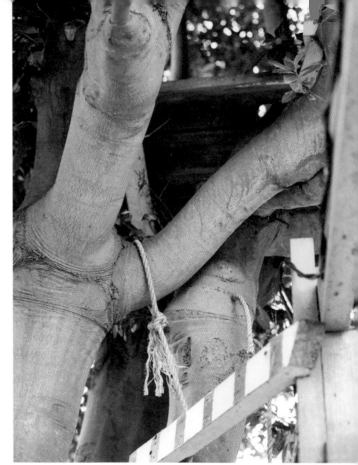

In 2015 they designed the Espresso Library, a café with vintage industrial lights and racing bicycles hanging from the ceiling (opposite). The look is more Shoreditch than Cambridge and, as in their own home, Vanessa and Brendan used almost-white wallpapers – 'Industrial Drawers' and 'Bookshelf' – to contrast with the concrete walls. Mid-century furniture and a black-painted wall with a cycle map of Cambridge complete the look. The space also doubles up as an office for the couple, who regularly bring clients here.

As she is always rushing from nursery to work and home again, Vanessa painted a list on the back of her bathroom door to remind her to 'make one thing a day, walk more and unplug more' (p. 277). Maintaining a work-life balance is difficult with a young family, and the couple escape the pressures of work by going out on bike rides with their dog Lili. 'You can cycle or walk everywhere,' Vanessa says. 'It's not too far to get to open fields with cows and horses, which Antonio loves.'

Directory

**VANESSA BATTAGLIA
& BRENDAN YOUNG**

Designers, pp. 276–85
Studio: 30 High Street, Fenstanton,
Cambridgeshire PE28 9JZ
Espresso Library: 210 East Road,
Cambridge CB1 1BG
mineheart.com
espressolibrary.com
youngbattaglia.com

LOUISE BODY

Wallpaper designer, pp. 256–65
Studio: 20 Caves Road,
St Leonards-on-Sea,
East Sussex TN38 0BY
louisebody.com

**CHARLOTTE BOYENS
& ADAM SCOTT**

Architects, pp. 142–53
High Haven, Lambston,
Haverfordwest,
Pembrokeshire SA62 3LR
freestate.co.uk

IVOR BRAKA

Art dealer, pp. 38–47
Gunton Arms, Cromer Road,
Thorpe Market, Norwich,
Norfolk NR11 8TZ
theguntonarms.co.uk

DANIEL & JULIET CHADWICK

Artists, pp. 28–37
The Woolpack Inn,
Slad Road, Slad, Stroud,
Gloucestershire GL6 7QA
thewoolpackslad.com
danielchadwick.com
julietchadwick.com

ZARA CHANCELLOR

Painter, pp. 86–95
zarachancellor.com

HELEN & COLIN DAVID

Artists, pp. 48–57
helenandcolindavid.com

**SARAH FEATHERSTONE
& JEREMY YOUNG**

Architects, pp. 122–31
Ty Hedfan, Pontfaen, Brecon,
Powys LD3 9RR
Studio: 25 Links Yard, Spelman Street,
London E1 5LX
ty-hedfan.co.uk
featherstoneyoung.com

JO FLOWERS

Florist and stylist, pp. 238–47
Colney, Norfolk NR4 7TY
joflowers.co.uk
instagram.com/joflowers

DUNCAN JACKSON

Industrial designer, pp. 132–41
billingsjackson.com

REIKO KANEKO

Ceramicist, pp. 158–65
Studio: Unit 8 Marie Works,
Ayshford Street,
Stoke-on-Trent,
Staffordshire ST3 2PP
reikokaneko.co.uk

**BEN LANGLANDS
& NIKKI BELL**

Artists, pp. 76–85
langlandsandbell.com

SALLY MACKERETH
Architect, pp. 100–9
Studio: 7b St Pancras Way,
London NW1 0PB
studiomackereth.com
instagram.com/ceramicsjv

PHILIP OAKLEY
Illuminations, pp. 228–37
Showroom: The Admiral Benbow,
2 London Road, St Leonards-on-Sea,
East Sussex TN37 6AE
oakleyilluminations.co.uk

JO PILKINGTON
Vintage caravans, pp. 266–75
The Old Rectory, Brampton Abbotts,
Ross-on-Wye, Herefordshire HR9 7JE
maddogsandvintagevans.co.uk

LUKE POWELL
Shipwright, pp. 196–205
Working Sail: 28 St Thomas Street,
Penryn, Cornwall TR10 8JN
workingsail.co.uk

GREG POWLESLAND
Shipwright, pp. 176–85
Tremerlin, Penarvon, Helford,
Helston, Cornwall TR12 6JZ
tremerlin.co.uk

CAMILA PRADA
Ceramicist, pp. 206–13
Studio: Unit 8 Roslyn Works,
Uttoxeter Road, Longton,
Stoke-on-Trent, Staffordshire ST3 1PQ
camilaprada.com

CHLOE & JIM READ
Clockmakers, pp. 166–75
Unit 3, Glovers Meadow, Oswestry,
Shropshire SY10 8NH
newgateclocks.com

AHMED SIDKI
Cabinetmaker, pp. 186–95
At The Chapel: High Street,
Bruton, Somerset BA10 0AE
atthechapel.co.uk
bowwow.co.uk

MATILDA TEMPERLEY
Photographer, pp. 58–67
Pass Vale Farm, Burrow Hill,
Kingsbury Episcopi, Martock,
Somerset TA12 6BU
matildatemperley.com

**JONATHAN WALTER
& LAKSHMI BHASKARAN**
Furniture designers, pp. 218–27
Bark: Bude, Cornwall EX23 9DW
barkfurniture.com

LISA WHATMOUGH
Designer, pp. 248–55
Shop: Studio 3 The Textile Building,
29a Chatham Place,
London E9 6FJ
squintlimited.com

**KATY WOOLLACOTT
& PATRICK GILMARTIN**
Architects, pp. 110–21
Studio: 48b Netherhall Gardens,
London NW3 5RG
woollacottgilmartin.com

HARRY CORY WRIGHT
Photographer, pp. 68–75
Represented by: Eleven,
11 Eccleston Street,
London SW1W 9LX
harrycorywright.com
elevenfineart.com

Travelling around the countryside was made a hundred times easier
by the support of our great friend Lucy Geering and GWR. Thanks also
to our families (Paul, Ella, Kate, Jude and Belle) for encouraging us in
our exploration of boats, towers and chapels around the UK.

with over 400 illustrations

On the cover: *front* Patrick Gilmartin at his converted mill house in the
Welsh countryside; *back, clockwise from top left* An artwork by Colin
David; Phil Oakley outside his front door in Hastings; Reiko Kaneko's
ceramics studio in Staffordshire; Ty Hedfan, the house in Wales designed
by architects Sarah Featherstone and Jeremy Young.

First published in the United Kingdom in 2017 by
Thames & Hudson Ltd, 181A High Holborn, London WC1V 7QX

British Library Cataloguing-in-Publication Data
A catalogue record for this book is available from the British Library

ISBN 978-0-500-51909-7

Printed and bound in China by C & C Offset Printing Co. Ltd

To find out about all our publications, please visit **www.thamesandhudson.com**.
There you can subscribe to our e-newsletter, browse or download our current
catalogue, and buy any titles that are in print.